Dinner time

MB
MACAW
BOOKS

© Macaw Books

www.macawbooks.com

Printed in India

It was dinner time, and Lily was very hungry. 'Grr!' rumbled her tummy, and Lily giggled.

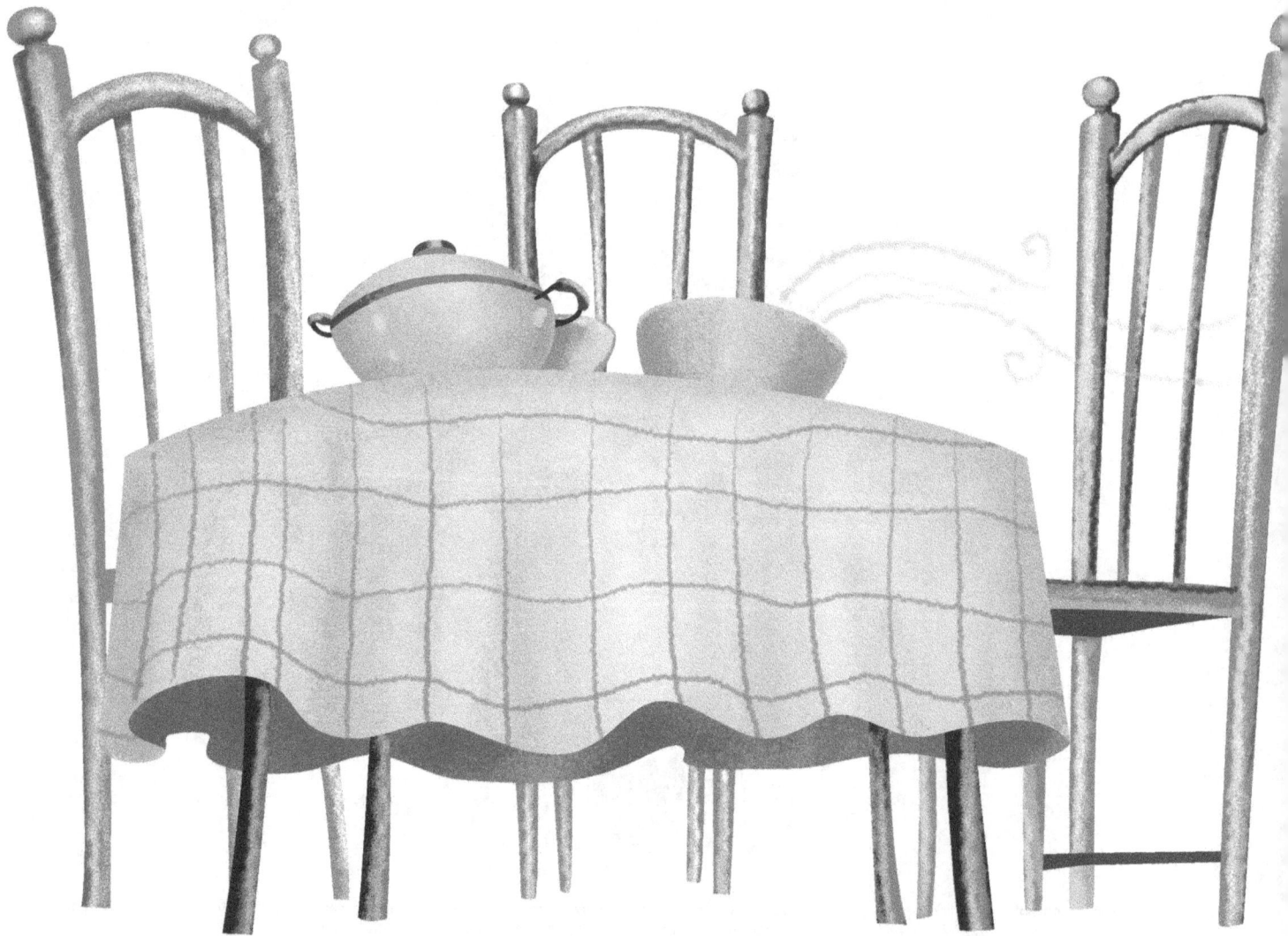

She washed her hands and went to the dining table.

'The food smells so yummy, Mummy!' said Lily.

Lily put the napkin on her lap and sat straight at the table. She grinned widely.

She waited as Mummy put her food onto her plate.

At first, Mummy put some eggs, mushroom and rice in Lily's plate. 'I can smell chicken!' said Lily.

Sure enough, there was chicken too. Lily loved the chicken that Mummy cooked. It was her favourite dish.

Lily was very polite at the dinner table. She always remembered her table manners.

When she wanted anything she always said, "Please.'
Mummy was happy that Lily was enjoying her food.

Lily took small bites. She did not chew with her mouth open. She chewed slowly with her mouth closed.
And she did not talk until she had swallowed her food.

Lily did not eat too fast and
she did not waste any food.
She ate slowly and finished
all her vegetables! When
she finished eating, she
wiped her mouth carefully
with her napkin.

Lily was very happy at the end of the meal. She felt very grateful for the good food that she had eaten.

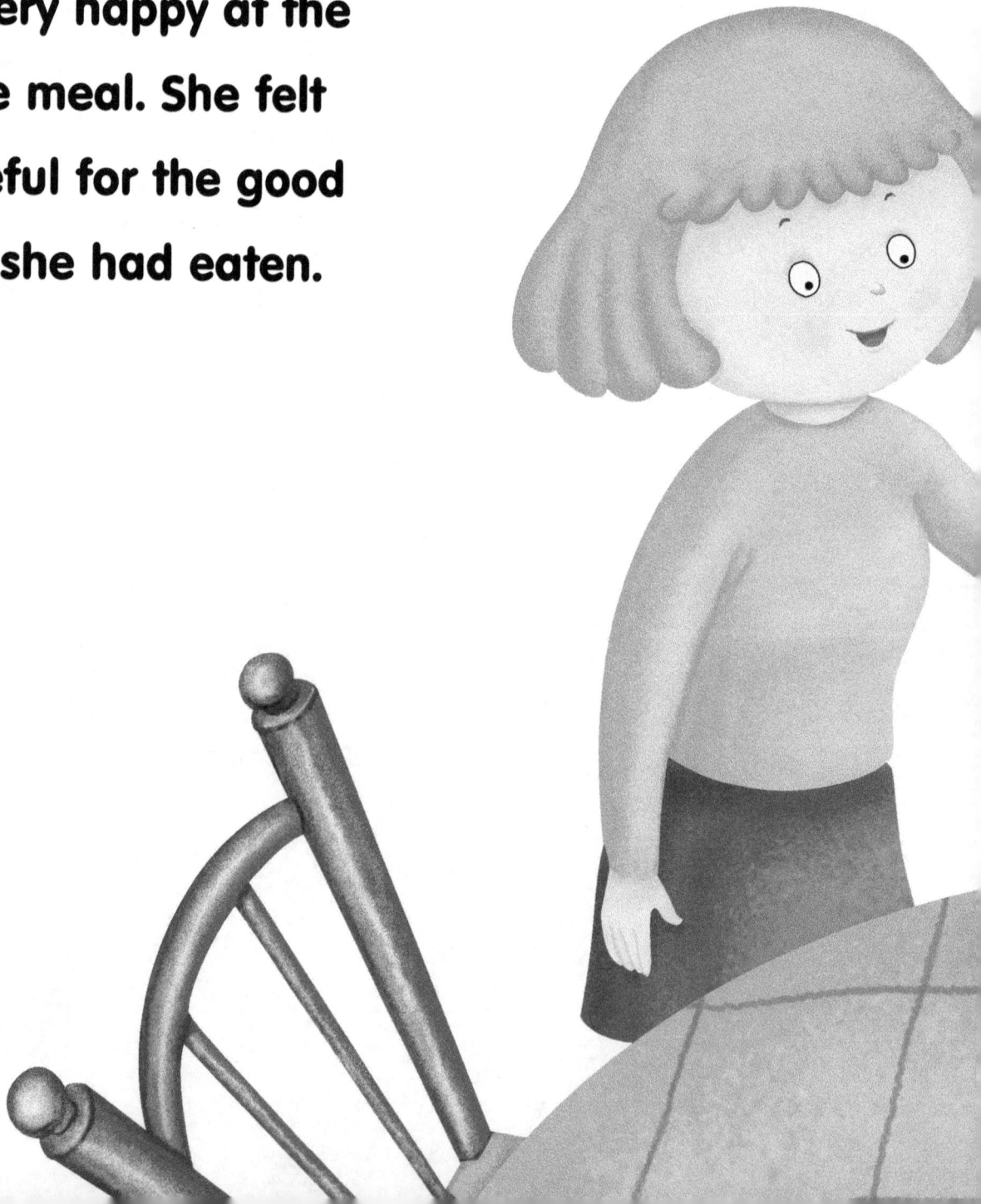

She thanked Mummy for cooking such a lovely meal. Lily climbed down from the chair and helped Mummy clear the table.

'What a delicious meal I have had!' said Lily. Her stomach was full, and she felt as glad as she could be!

when i grow up

Mummy asked Abby one day, 'Abby, what do you want to be when you grow up?'

'I can be anything mummy. Why do you worry?'
Little Abby's daddy looked at her in wonder.

Abby said, 'Daddy I can be an astronaut. I will fly in a rocket and see the stars.'

'Or I can be an athlete. I can be the fastest runner in the world.'

Little Abby knew she can be anything. She can be a fireman saving people and pets from fire.

She can be a hatter and make beautiful hats. She can make hats for all her friends.

She can be a zookeeper. She can
take care of all the lovely animals.'

Abby can be a doctor, nurse or vet. She
can take care of sick people or animals.

Abby can be a racer. She can drive racing cars and win many races.

'But Mummy, I wonder if I can be a pirate,' asked Abby. Mummy said, 'Pirates are not nice. You can be a sailor and sail across oceans.'

Abby thought for a while and said, 'I can be a postman and bring letters to daddy.'

'Or I can design beautiful clothes for everyone.
I can be a seamstress and sew clothes.'

Abby looked at the flowers in the garden and said, 'I can be a florist and sell flowers.'

'Or I will be a movie star. Every one will watch me in the theatre.'

Mummy and Daddy are so happy. They know that little Abby can grow up to be anything that she want to.

9 781640 358034